KEY STAGE 1
Maths

Write your name in the space below.

This book belongs to:

GW00419772

Encourage your child to practise their maths skills, earning a gold star reward after completing each page!

Getting Started

Sit at a table or desk. This book is designed for your child to work through with an adult. Encourage your child to read the instructions out loud and ask any questions. Talk about each activity and praise both your child's effort and their achievement. The activities are designed to be fun and enjoyable and should be completed at your child's pace. There are answers at the back of the book.

Things To Do

- Work through the pages in order, completing all the activities before moving on to the next page.
- The gold star sticker will cover the page number. Check the answers and then ask your child to place a gold star at the bottom of each page.
- Use a pencil and rub or cross out any wrong answers.
- Photocopy pages if you want to use them again at home. There are extra gold star stickers to use on photocopied pages, or to create your own reward chart.

This book includes the following topics:

- Number bonds
- Counting
- Addition
- Subtraction
- Tens and ones
- Times tables
- Shapes
- Fractions
- Money
- Time

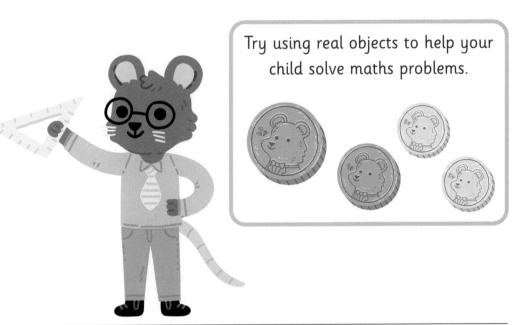

Try using real objects to help your child solve maths problems.

Text: Emily Stead
Illustrations: Lizzy Doyle
Editor: Emily Stead
Design: Rachel Baines
Series editor: Emma Munro Smith
Creative Director: Anton Poitier
Educational consultants: Libby Kean BA (Hons) Ed,
Tony Potter PhD, BEd (Hons), Cert Ed,
Sara McInnes BA (Hons) Ed

Copyright © 2020 iSeek Ltd.
1A Stairbridge Court, Haywards Heath,
West Sussex, RH17 5PA, UK.
All rights reserved.
Printed in the EU

Number words

Draw a line to match the numeral with the right number word. The first one has been done for you.

1		five
2		one
3		six
4		two
5		three
6		four
7		ten
8		seven
9		eight
10		nine

You know your numbers! Add your first gold star sticker.

3

Adding numbers

We use the + sign when we add amounts or numbers together. Complete the number sentences below by adding the things and the numbers together.

Use the number line at the bottom of the page if you need help.

+ 2 = ☐

+ 5 = ☐

Look at the number sentences below. What do you notice?

3 + 4 = ☐   5 + 1 = ☐

4 + 3 = ☐   1 + 5 = ☐

It doesn't matter in which order you add the same numbers, the total will be the same.

4

Clever counting! Add your next gold star sticker.

Adding numbers

Complete these number sentences. Write the answer in the box.

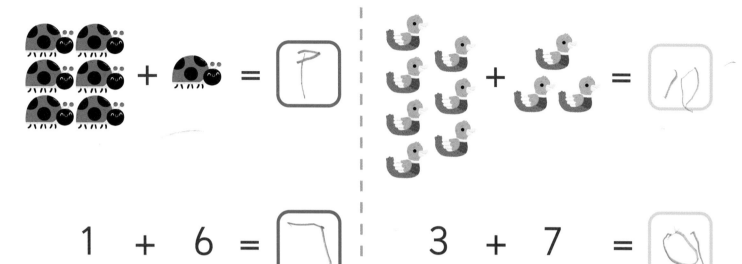

1 + 6 = [7]

3 + 7 = [10]

Colour the starfish blue and red to show two different ways to make the same number. The first one shows you how.

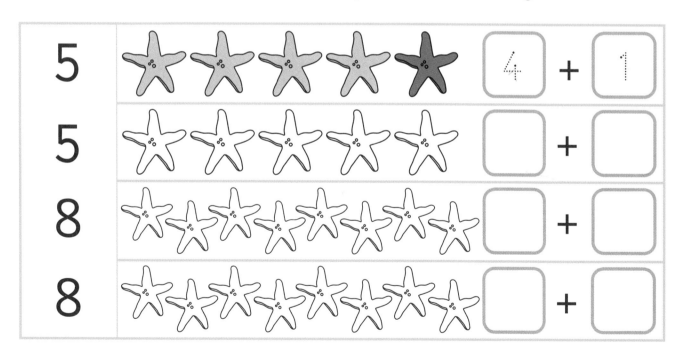

Number bonds to 10

Number bonds are pairs of numbers that add together to make a certain number. Add the same colour fish in one bowl to the same colour fish in the other bowl to make 10.

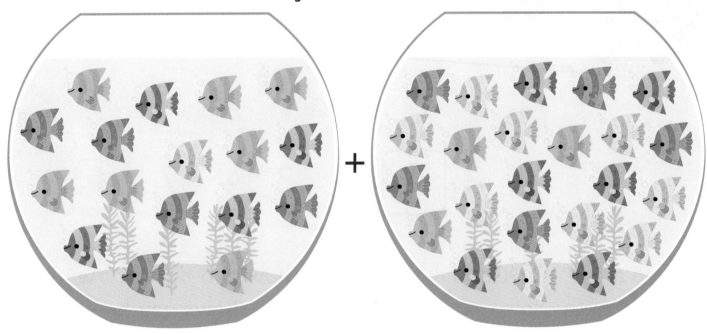

Count the fish in each bowl. Fill in each number.

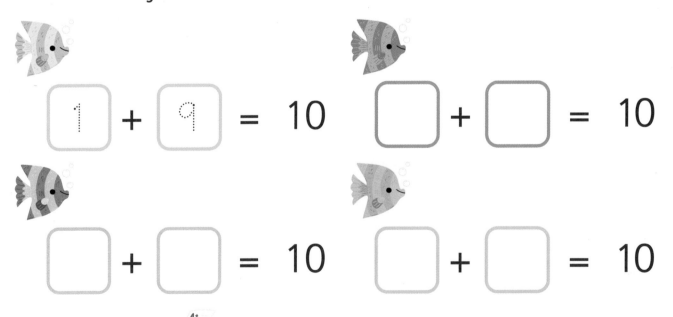

$1 + 9 = 10$

$\square + \square = 10$

$\square + \square = 10$

$\square + \square = 10$

6

Note to parent: Number bonds are sometimes called 'number families'. They are groups of numbers that make up a given number.

One more, one less

Fill in the missing numbers on the eggs by finding one more and one less. Use the number line to help you.

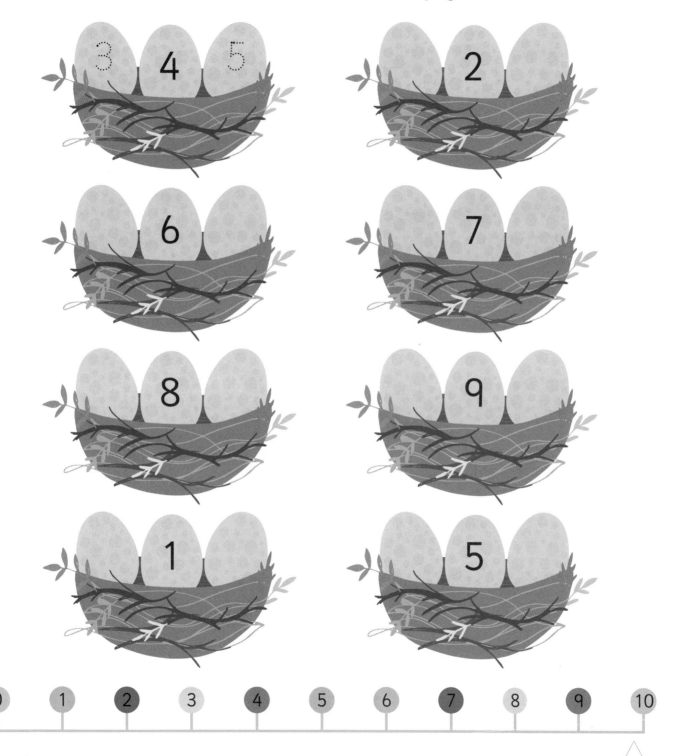

Subtracting numbers

Subtraction is where we take away one number from another number. We use the − sign when we subtract numbers.

5   −   2   =   3

To subtract 2 from 5 using the number line, start at 5, then hop back two numbers. The answer is 3.

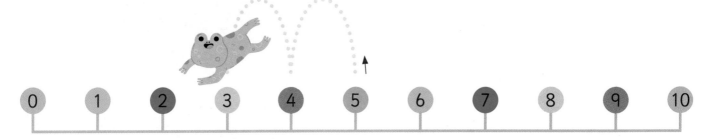

Use the number line to help you work out these number sentences. Count back each time.

−   =

8   −   4   =

8

Super subtractions! Add a gold sticker for your hard work.

Subtracting numbers

Use the number lines to help with these subtractions.
Colour in the fruit to show your answer.

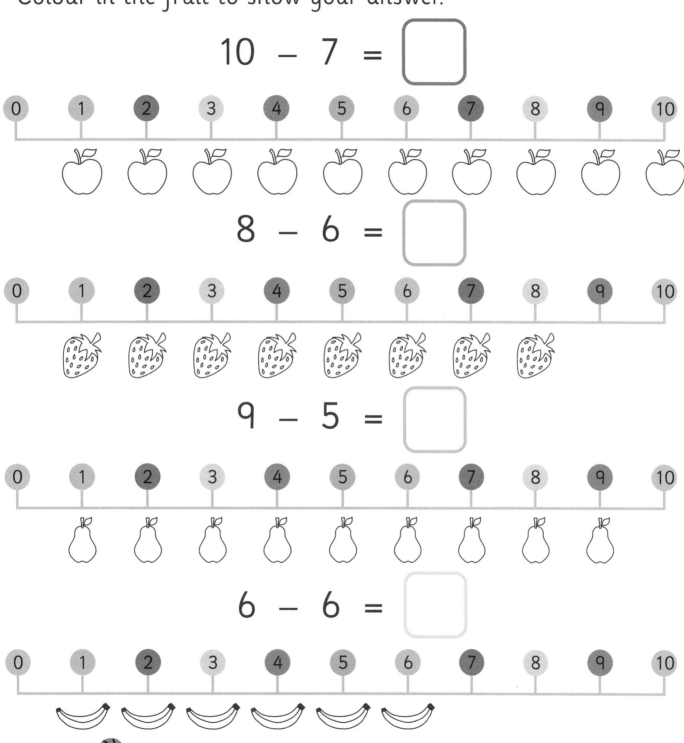

10 – 7 =

8 – 6 =

9 – 5 =

6 – 6 =

Great work! Add a sticker for your hard work.

9

Adding numbers

Count the things then write the number sentence. Use the number line at the bottom of the page to help you.

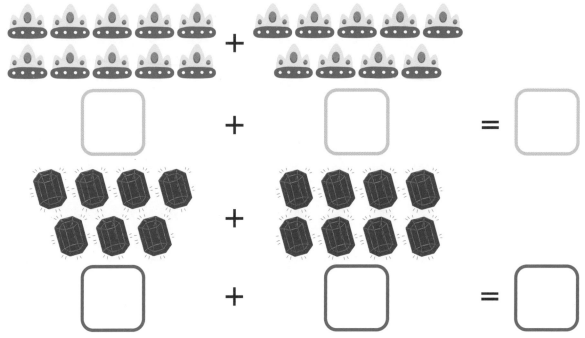

Write the answers to these addition number sentences. The first one has been done for you.

18 + 1 = [19]   20 + 0 = [ ]

6 + 6 = [ ]   10 + 5 = [ ]

17 + 3 = [ ]   4 + 9 = [ ]

0 1 2 3 4 5 6 7 8 9 10 11 12 13 14 15 16 17 18 19 20

Excellent addition! Add your next gold star sticker.

Subtracting numbers below 20

Solve these subtraction problems.
Write each number sentence in the boxes underneath.

Bear made 18 sandwiches for his party. 11 get eaten. How many are left? Cross out the sandwiches to find the answer.

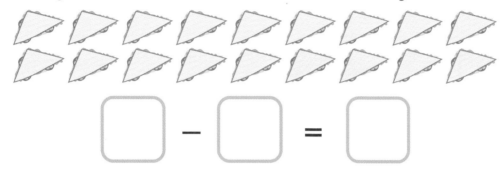

☐ − ☐ = ☐

Bear made 20 cupcakes for his party. 17 get eaten. How many are left? Cross out the cakes to find the answer.

☐ − ☐ = ☐

Now try these subtraction number sentences.
The first one has been done for you.

18 − 3 = 15   19 − 8 = ☐

20 − 5 = ☐   16 − 4 = ☐

Tens and ones

Split these 2-digit numbers into group of tens and ones.
The first one has been done for you.

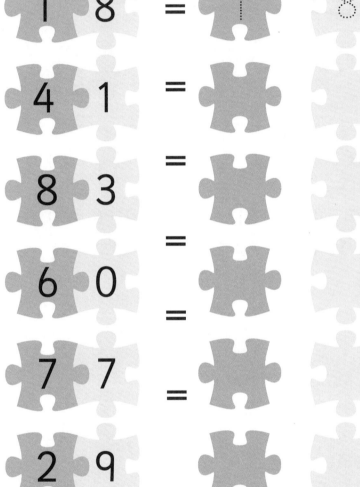

tens   ones

1 8 = 1   8

There is 1 group of tens and 8 ones in the number 18.

4 1 =

8 3 =

6 0 =

7 7 =

2 9 =

Circle the numbers that have 5 ones.

| 75 | 54 | 35 | 31 | 85 | 17 | 15 |

Terrific tens and wonderful ones! Add a gold star sticker.

Tens and ones

Count the groups of tens and ones, then write the total in the box.

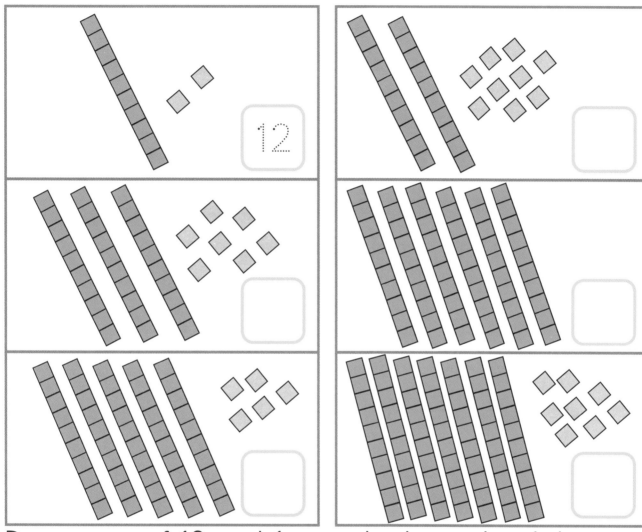

Draw groups of 10s and 1s to make the numbers below.

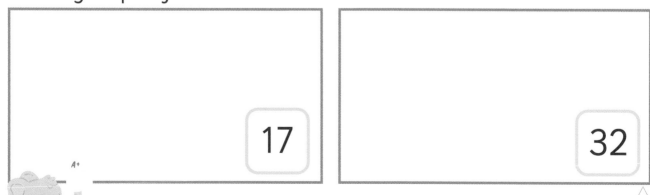

Counting in twos

Fill in the missing numbers by counting in twos and help the otter find the umbrella.

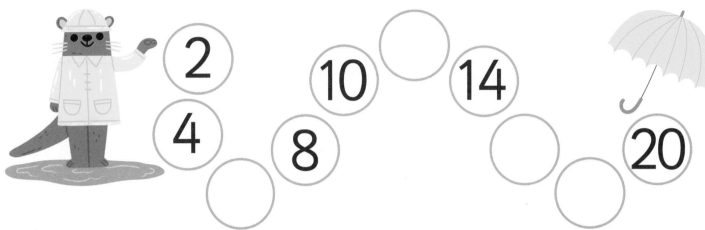

This time, count backwards in twos. Help the kangaroo jump back to its baby by filling in the missing numbers.

Great counting! Add your next gold star sticker.

Counting in fives and tens

Now let's count in fives. Fill in the missing numbers.
What do you notice about how the numbers end?

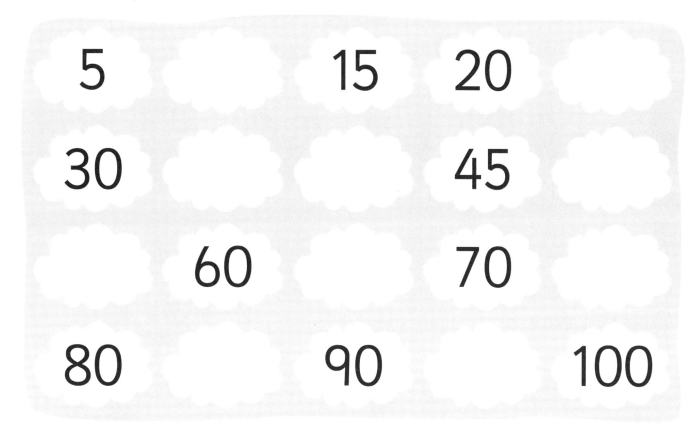

5   15   20

30   45

60   70

80   90   100

Now count in tens. Fill in the missing numbers.
What do you notice about these numbers?

10   30   40

70   100

High five! Add another gold star.

Two times table

Multiplying a number is the same as adding the same number lots of times.

When we multiply numbers we use the x sign.

$4 \times 2 = 8$ is the same as:

Four lots of two equals eight.

Times tables help us to count in groups of the same number.
For the 2 x table, we count in groups of 2.
Count in twos and fill in the answers.

1 x 2 = ☐   7 x 2 = ☐

2 x 2 = ☐   8 x 2 = ☐

3 x 2 = ☐   9 x 2 = ☐

4 x 2 = ☐   10 x 2 = ☐

5 x 2 = ☐   11 x 2 = ☐

6 x 2 = ☐   12 x 2 = ☐

16   Fantastic! Add your next gold star.

Two times table

Finish the number sentences. Count the animals and times each number by two. Write the answer in the box.

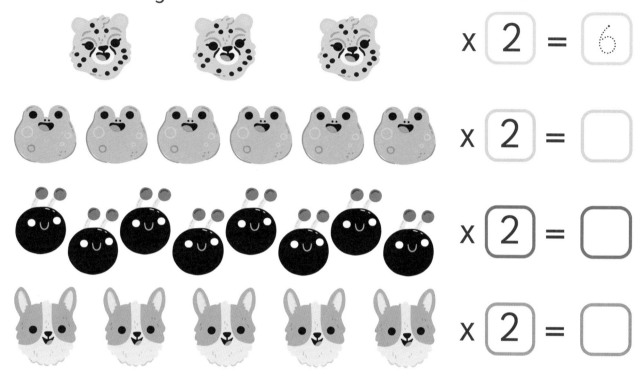

x 2 = 6

x 2 = ☐

x 2 = ☐

x 2 = ☐

Take the 2 x table challenge! Colour only the numbers that appear in the 2 x table. The first one has been done for you.

1	2	3	4	5
6	7	8	9	10
11	12	13	14	15
16	17	18	19	20
21	22	23	24	25

Five times table

Now let's count in sets of 5.
Colour only the numbers in the grid that are multiples of 5.

1	2	3	4	5	6	7	8	9	10
11	12	13	14	15	16	17	18	19	20
21	22	23	24	25	26	27	28	29	30
31	32	33	34	35	36	37	38	39	40
41	42	43	44	45	46	47	48	49	50

Fill in the answers to the five times table.

1 x 5 = ☐   7 x 5 = ☐

2 x 5 = ☐   8 x 5 = ☐

3 x 5 = ☐   9 x 5 = ☐

4 x 5 = ☐   10 x 5 = ☐

5 x 5 = ☐   11 x 5 = ☐

6 x 5 = ☐   12 x 5 = ☐

Terrific times tables work! Add a gold star sticker.

Five times table

Count the things and solve these number sentences.

x 5 = ☐

x 5 = ☐

x 5 = ☐

Join the dots in the order of the 5 x table.
What can you see?

55   60   5   10

50   15

45   20

40   25

35   30

Well done! Add your next gold star sticker.

Ten times table

For the 10 x table, we count in groups of 10. Count in 10s and fill in the missing numbers to help the bears get home.

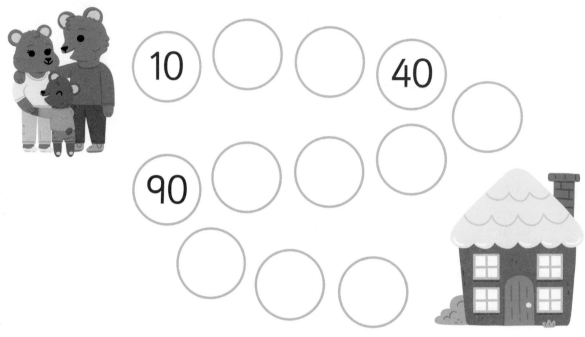

Fill in the answers to the ten times table.

1 x 10 =

2 x 10 =

3 x 10 =

4 x 10 =

5 x 10 =

6 x 10 =

7 x 10 =

8 x 10 =

9 x 10 =

10 x 10 =

11 x 10 =

12 x 10 =

Easy-peasy! Add your next gold star sticker.

Ten times table

Colour only the numbers in the grid that appear in the 10 x table. What do you notice?

1	2	3	4	5	6	7	8	9	10
11	12	13	14	15	16	17	18	19	20
21	22	23	24	25	26	27	28	29	30
31	32	33	34	35	36	37	38	39	40
41	42	43	44	45	46	47	48	49	50
51	52	53	54	55	56	57	58	59	60
61	62	63	64	65	66	67	68	69	70
71	72	73	74	75	76	77	78	79	80
81	82	83	84	85	86	87	88	89	90
91	92	93	94	95	96	97	98	99	100

Count the animals and solve the number sentences.

$\square$ x 10 = $\square$

$\square$ x 10 = $\square$

$\square$ x 10 = $\square$

Excellent numbers work! Add another gold star.

Halves

When something is divided into two equal parts, we call each part a half. Colour half of each shape.

We also write a half as $\frac{1}{2}$. Tick the shapes that show a $\frac{1}{2}$.

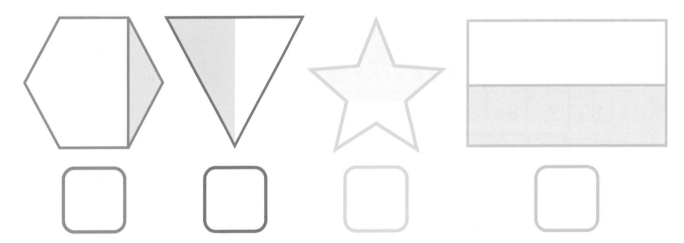

Draw a circle around exactly half the footballs.

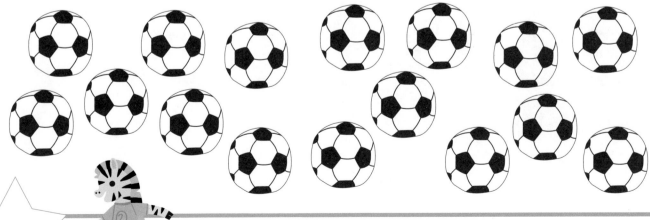

Well done! Add another gold star sticker.

Quarters

These shapes are split into 4 equal parts, called quarters.
Colour the shapes to match the descriptions below.

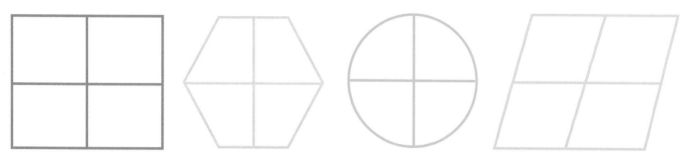

one quarter   two quarters   three quarters   four quarters

We also write a quarter as $\frac{1}{4}$.

Draw lines to divide these foods into four equal quarters.

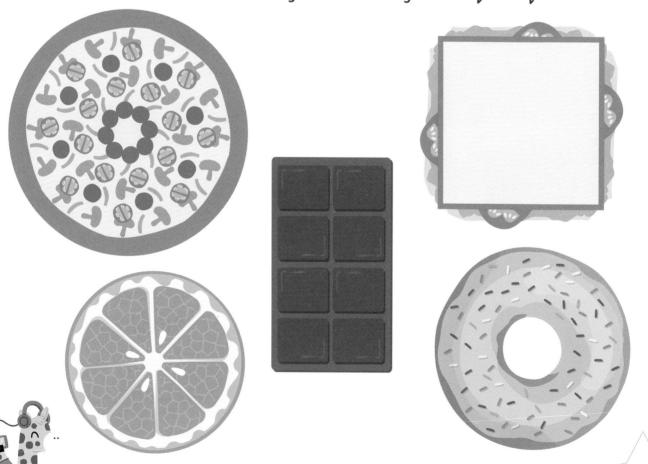

Measuring size

Find the longest, shortest, and biggest. Then look at the ruler showing centimetres.

Circle the longest snake.

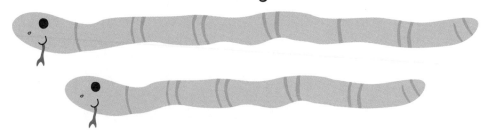

Circle the shortest tree.

Circle the biggest elephant.

Use this ruler to measure your thumb. Each number is a centimetre. Write down how long your thumb is below.

My thumb is: ____ centimetres.

What else could you measure?

Symmetry

Something is symmetrical when it is the same on both sides. Draw and colour these pictures so that both sides match.

Draw a line of symmetry on each of these shapes to split them into equal halves. The first shape shows you how.

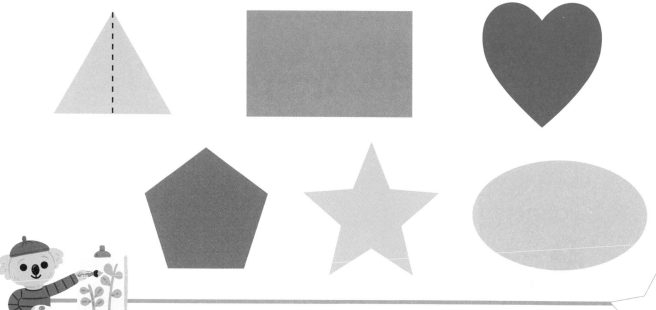

Great work! Add another gold star.

2D shapes

Can you name these 2D shapes?
Write the names, then count the sides and corners.

....

sides ☐

corners ☐

....

sides ☐

corners ☐

....

sides ☐

corners ☐

....

sides ☐

corners ☐

....

sides ☐

corners ☐

26

Note to parent: Schools may teach the word 'vertices' instead of 'corners' (the points where two or more sides meet).

3D shapes

3D shapes are solid objects with faces and edges. Join each 3D shape to its name. Trace the dots to write the name.

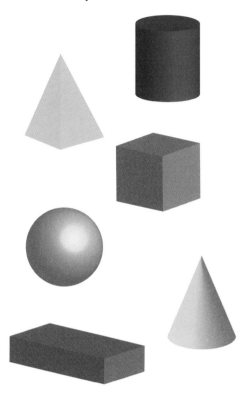

cube

pyramid

cuboid

cylinder

cone

sphere

Colour the picture using the key. Write the name of each shape.

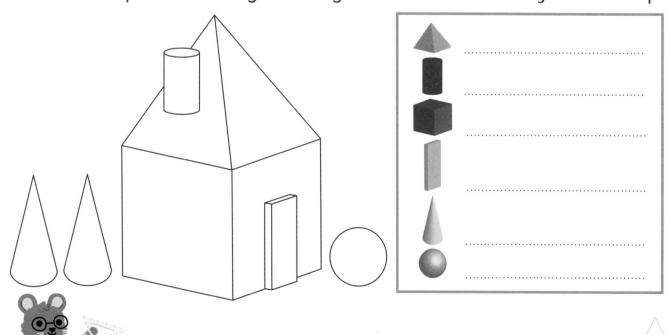

....

....

....

....

....

....

Counting money

Add up the coins in each piggy bank and write the total.

total = ☐ p

total = ☐ p

total = ☐ p

total = ☐ p

Draw the coins you need to make the totals.

32 p

41 p

Well done! Add your next gold star sticker.

Counting money

Read the menu to work out how much each ice cream costs.
Then draw the coins you need.

Ice Cream Menu
1 scoop = 10p
2 scoops = 20p
3 scoops = 30p
4 scoops = 40p
flake = 10p
sauce = 4p

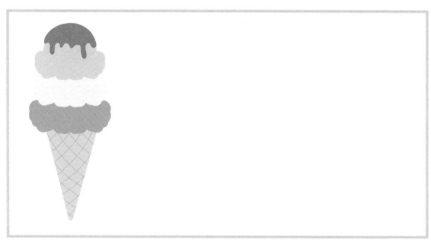

1p   2p

5p   10p

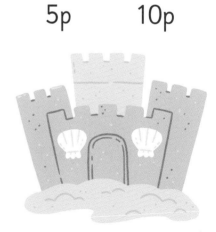

Excellent counting! You have earned your next gold star.

Telling the time

We use clocks to keep track of the time.
This clock shows 3 o'clock.

The long hand is called the minute hand. It shows how many minutes have passed.

The short hand is called the hour hand. It shows what hour it is.

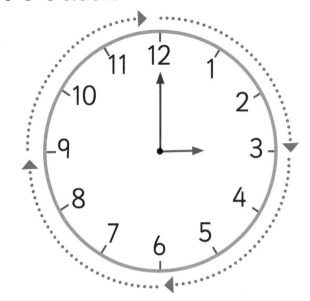

The numbers 1 to 12 on a clock go in a clockwise direction.

When the minute hand points to 12, we say the time is **o'clock**. The hour hand shows the hour.
Draw the hour hand on each clock below to show the right time.

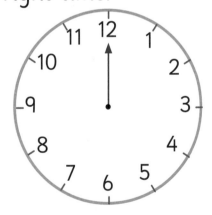

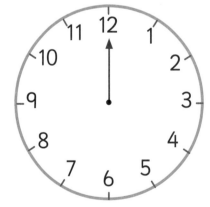

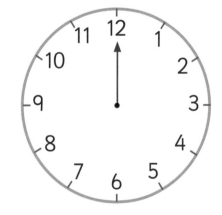

6 **o'clock**   2 **o'clock**   10 **o'clock**

Do you have a clock at home? Try to tell the time using it.

Telling the time

Write the correct time below each clock.

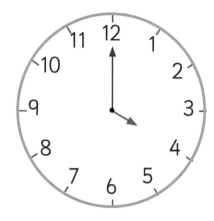

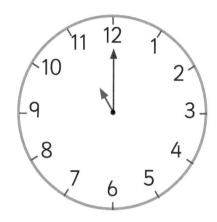

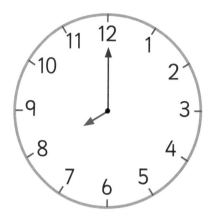

o'clock

.... | .... | ....

When the minute
hand points to the
number 6, the time
is half past the hour.

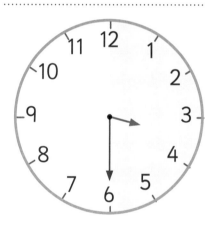

The time on this
clock is half past 3.
The hour hand
points halfway
between the 3 and
the 4.

Draw the minute hand on each clock to show the correct time.

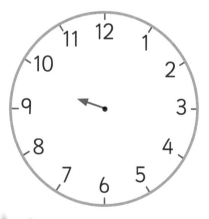

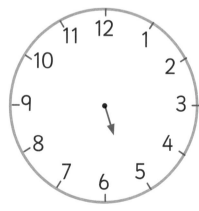

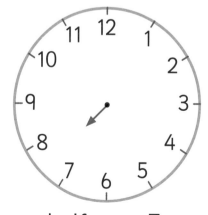

half past 9

half past 5

half past 7

Well done! Add your next gold star sticker.

31

Answers

Page 3
1 - five
2 - one
3 - six
4 - two
5 - three
6 - four
7 - ten
8 - seven
9 - eight
10 - nine

Page 4
$3 + 2 = 5$ $3 + 5 = 8$

$3 + 4 = 7$ $5 + 1 = 6$
$4 + 3 = 7$ $1 + 5 = 6$

Page 5
$6 + 1 = 7$ $7 + 3 = 10$
$1 + 6 = 7$ $3 + 7 = 10$

5	★★★★★	4 + 1	or
5		3 + 2	5+0
8		4 + 4	7+1
8		5 + 3	6+2

Page 6
yellow $1 + 9 = 10$ pink $5 + 5 = 10$
blue $4 + 6 = 10$ green $7 + 3 = 10$

Page 7
5, 6, 7; 7, 8, 9, 0, 1, 2
1, 2, 3; 6, 7, 8; 8, 9; 10; 4, 5, 6

Page 8
$4 - 4 = 0$ $8 - 4 = 4$

Page 9
$10 - 7 = 3$ 3 coloured apples
$8 - 6 = 2$ 2 coloured strawberries
$9 - 5 = 4$ 4 coloured pears
$6 - 6 = 0$ 0 coloured bananas

Page 10
$10 + 9 = 19$ $7 + 8 = 15$

                          $20 + 0 = 20$
$6 + 6 = 12$ $10 + 5 = 15$
$17 + 3 = 20$ $4 + 9 = 13$

Page 11

$18 - 11 = 7$

$20 - 17 = 3$

$20 - 5 = 15$ $19 - 8 = 11$
                          $16 - 4 = 12$

Page 12
$4 + 1$
$8 + 3$
$6 + 0$
$7 + 7$
$2 + 9$
75, 35, 85, 15

Page 13

12	29
37	60
55	78
17	32

Page 14
2, 4, ,6 ,8, 10, 12, 14, 16, 18, 20
24, 22, 20, 18, 16, 14, 12, 10, 8, 6, 4, 2

Page 15

5	10	15	20	25
30	35	40	45	50
55	60	65	70	75
80	85	90	95	100

| 10 | 20 | 30 | 40 | 50 |
| 60 | 70 | 80 | 90 | 100 |

Page 16
$1 \times 2 = 2$ $7 \times 2 = 14$
$2 \times 2 = 4$ $8 \times 2 = 16$
$3 \times 2 = 6$ $9 \times 2 = 18$
$4 \times 2 = 8$ $10 \times 2 = 20$
$5 \times 2 = 10$ $11 \times 2 = 22$
$6 \times 2 = 12$ $12 \times 2 = 24$

Page 17
$3 \times 2 = 6$
$6 \times 2 = 12$
$8 \times 2 = 16$
$5 \times 2 = 10$

1	2	3	4	5
6	7	8	9	10
11	12	13	14	15
16	17	18	19	20
21	22	23	24	25

Page 18

1	2	3	4	5	6	7	8	9	10
11	12	13	14	15	16	17	18	19	20
21	22	23	24	25	26	27	28	29	30
31	32	33	34	35	36	37	38	39	40
41	42	43	44	45	46	47	48	49	50

$1 \times 5 = 5$ $7 \times 5 = 35$
$2 \times 5 = 10$ $8 \times 5 = 40$
$3 \times 5 = 15$ $9 \times 5 = 45$
$4 \times 5 = 20$ $10 \times 5 = 50$
$5 \times 5 = 25$ $11 \times 5 = 55$
$6 \times 5 = 30$ $12 \times 5 = 60$

Page 19
$5 \times 5 = 25$, $7 \times 5 = 35$, $6 \times 5 = 30$

Page 20

$1 \times 10 = 10$ $7 \times 10 = 70$
$2 \times 10 = 20$ $8 \times 10 = 80$
$3 \times 10 = 30$ $9 \times 10 = 90$
$4 \times 10 = 40$ $10 \times 10 = 100$
$5 \times 10 = 50$ $11 \times 10 = 110$
$6 \times 10 = 60$ $12 \times 10 = 120$

Page 21

1	2	3	4	5	6	7	8	9	10
11	12	13	14	15	16	17	18	19	20
21	22	23	24	25	26	27	28	29	30
31	32	33	34	35	36	37	38	39	40
41	42	43	44	45	46	47	48	49	50
51	52	53	54	55	56	57	58	59	60
61	62	63	64	65	66	67	68	69	70
71	72	73	74	75	76	77	78	79	80
81	82	83	84	85	86	87	88	89	90
91	92	93	94	95	96	97	98	99	100

$5 \times 10 = 50$, $6 \times 10 = 60$, $3 \times 10 = 30$

Page 22

rectangle, triangle

Page 23

Page 24

Page 25

Page 26
circle: 1 side, 0 corners
square: 4 sides, 4 corners
triangle: 3 sides, 3 corners
hexagon: 6 sides, 6 corners
oval: 1 side, 0 corners

Page 27
cube
pyramid
cuboid
cylinder
cone
sphere

pyramid
cylinder
cube
cuboid
cone
sphere

Page 28
44p   15p
8p   80p

Other coin combinations can be used.

Page 29

Page 30
6 o'clock   2 o'clock   10 o'clock

Page 31
4 o'clock, 11 o'clock, 8 o'clock

half-past 9   half-past 5   half-past 7

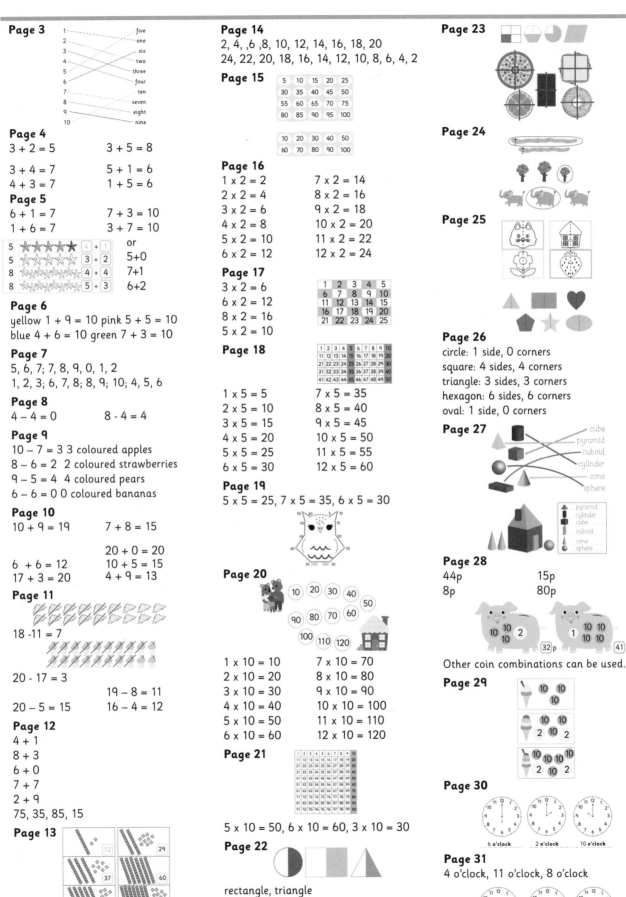